Little Pebble™

Healthy Me

I CARE FOR MY TEETH

by Martha E. H. Rustad

CAPSTONE PRESS
a capstone imprint

Little Pebble is published by Capstone Press,
1710 Roe Crest Drive, North Mankato, Minnesota 56003
www.mycapstone.com

Library of Congress Cataloging-in-Publication Data
Names: Rustad, Martha E. H. (Martha Elizabeth Hillman), 1975- author.
Title: I care for my teeth / by Martha E.H. Rustad.
Description: North Mankato, Minnesota : Capstone Press, [2017] | Series:
Little pebble. Healthy me | Audience: Age 4-7. | Audience: Grade K to grade 3. | Includes
bibliographical references and index.
Identifiers: LCCN 2016032847
ISBN 9781515739852 (library binding)
ISBN 9781515739890 (paperback)
ISBN 9781515740018 (eBook PDF)
Subjects: LCSH: Teeth—Care and hygiene—Juvenile literature. Dentistry—Juvenile literature.
Classification: LCC RK63 .R87 2017 | DDC 617.6—dc23
LC record available at https://lccn.loc.gov/2016032847

Editorial Credits
Shelly Lyons, editor; Juliette Peters, designer;
Jo Miller, media researcher; Tori Abraham, production specialist

Photo Credits
Images by Capstone Studio: Karon Dubke
Photo Styling: Sarah Schuette and Marcy Morin

Table of Contents

Brush!

Smile!

I want healthy teeth.

I brush my teeth twice a day.

I brush for two minutes.

I brush each tooth.

I floss.

I get the plaque out!

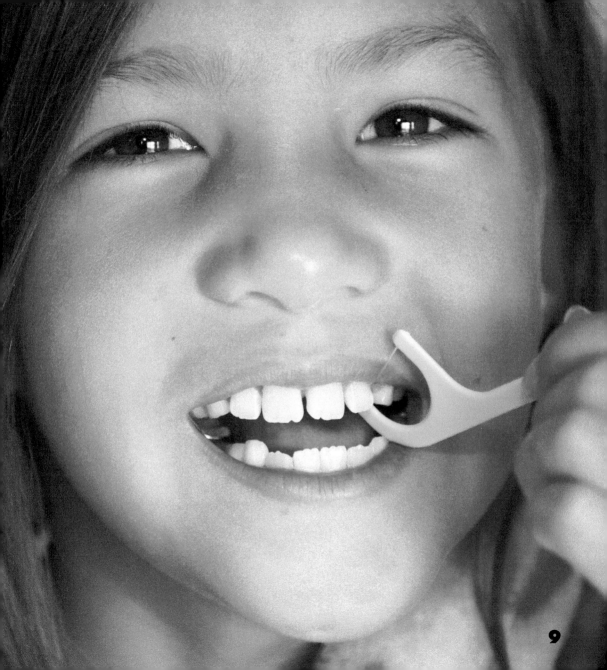

Food and Drinks

I eat healthful food.

Milk keeps my teeth strong.

Yum!

I drink water.

Sweet sodas hurt my teeth.

I brush after eating sweets.

If I can't brush, I rinse

with water.

Swish!

The Dentist

I go to the dentist's office.

She cleans my teeth.

I get a new toothbrush.

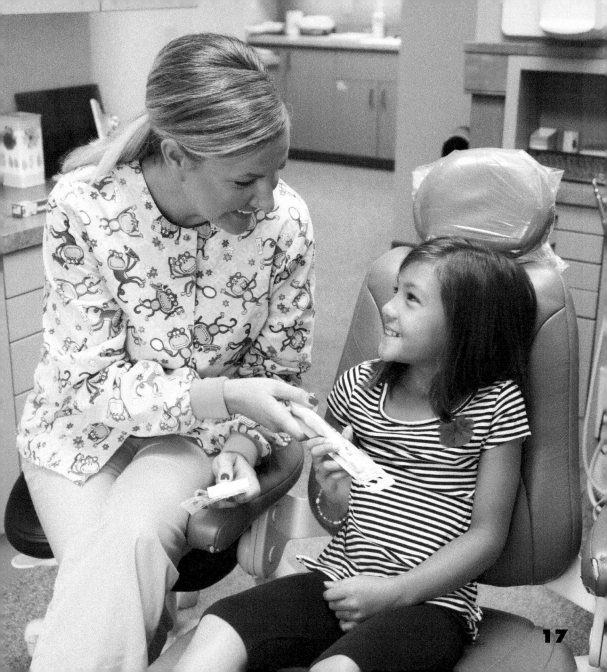

The dentist checks my mouth.

He looks at X-rays
of my teeth.

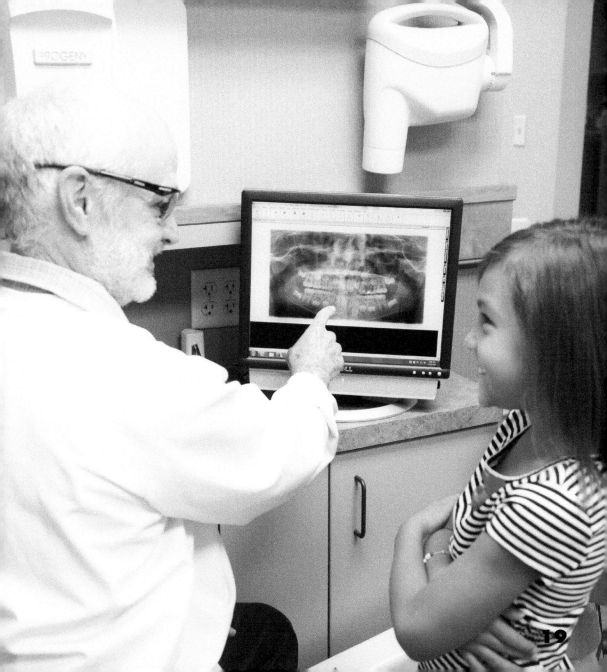

I care for my teeth.
Healthy teeth are part
of a healthy me!

Glossary

dentist—a doctor that takes care of teeth

floss—to clean between teeth with a thin string

healthful—having or helping to have good health

healthy—fit and well; not sick

plaque—a buildup on teeth that causes cavities, holes in teeth caused by decay or rotting

rinse—to wash with clean water

X-ray—a picture that looks inside your body; an X-ray of a mouth shows the roots of teeth

Read More

Herrington, Lisa M. *I Have a Cavity*. New York: Children's Press, 2015.

Salzmann, Mary Elizabeth. *Brush Your Teeth!: Healthy Dental Habits*. Healthy Habits. North Mankato, Minn.: Sandcastle, 2015.

Ziefert, Harriet. *Does a Tiger Go to the Dentist?: Think About How Teeth Stay Healthy*. Maplewood, N.J.: Blue Apple Books, 2014.

Internet Sites

FactHound offers a safe, fun way to find Internet sites related to this book. All of the sites on FactHound have been researched by our staff.

Here's all you do:
Visit *www.facthound.com*
Type in this code: 9781515739852

Super-cool stuff!

Check out projects, games and lots more at
www.capstonekids.com

Critical Thinking Using the Common Core

1. You should brush your teeth for how many minutes? (Key Ideas and Details)

2. Why do you think it is good to drink milk? (Integration of Knowledge and Ideas)

3. A dentist looks at X-rays. What are X-rays? (Craft and Structure)

Index